W9-ACM-235

Heart and Blood

Injury, Illness and Health

Carol Ballard

Heinemann Library
Chicago, Illinois

Customer Service 888-454-2279

Visit our website at www.heinemannlibrary.com

Originated by Ambassador Litho
Printed and bound in China by South China Printing Company

07 06 05 04 03
10 9 8 7 6 5 4 3 2 1

Library of Congress Cataloging-in-Publication Data
Ballard, Carol.
    The heart and blood / Carol Ballard.
        v. cm. -- (Body focus)
Includes bibliographical references and index.
Contents: The heart and circulatory system -- Healthy heart -- Heart structure -- Heart function -- Heart attack -- Heart monitoring -- Heart surgery -- Pace makers -- Faulty valves -- Heart transplant -- Blood vessels -- Problems with arteries -- Problems with veins -- Blood pressure -- Blood -- Blood groups -- Blood donors and blood transfusions -- Hemophilia -- Blood disorders -- Sickle cell anemia.
    ISBN 1-4034-0196-9 -- ISBN 1-4034-0452-6 (pbk.)
    1. Cardiovascular system--Juvenile literature. 2. Blood--Juvenile literature. [1. Circulatory system. 2. Blood.] I. Title. II. Series.
    QP103 .B355 2003
    612.1--dc21
                              2002014428

Acknowledgments
The publishers would like to thank the following for permission to reproduce photographs:
pp. 5, 17, 29, 36 Science Photo Library; p. 7 Science Photo Library/Simon Fraser/Newcastle General Hospital; p. 12 Stone/David Madison; p. 13 Corbis Stock Market/David Stoecklein; p. 14 Science Photo Library/Adam Hart-Davis; p. 16 Science Photo Library/Bisp Beranger; p. 18 Corbis Stock Market/Pete Saloutos; p. 22 (left) Mediscan; p. 22 (right) Steven Kahn; pp. 24, 25 Corbis Bettmann; p. 28 Science Photo Library/Alex Bartel; p. 31 Corbis Stock Market/John Henley; p. 33 Science Photo Library/Juergen Berger/Max-Planck Institute; p. 35 Corbis; p. 38 Science Photo Library/St. Bartholomew's Hospital; p. 40 Science Photo Library/Astrid & Hanns-Frieder Michler; p. 42 Science Photo Library/Jackie Lewin/Royal Free Hospital.

Cover photograph of a color X-ray image of a human heart reproduced with permission of Science Photo Library.

The publishers would like to thank David Wright for his assistance with the preparation of this book.

Every effort has been made to contact copyright holders of any material reproduced in this book. Any omissions will be rectified in subsequent printings if notice is given to the publishers.

Some words are shown in bold, **like this.** You can find out what they mean by looking in the glossary.

CONTENTS

THE HEART AND CIRCULATORY SYSTEM

The heart is a vital organ, pumping blood around our bodies every minute of every day of our lives. Blood is the body's main transport system. It carries oxygen and **nutrients** to tissues and removes waste products. Without a constant supply of blood, none of our organs would function, and we would soon die.

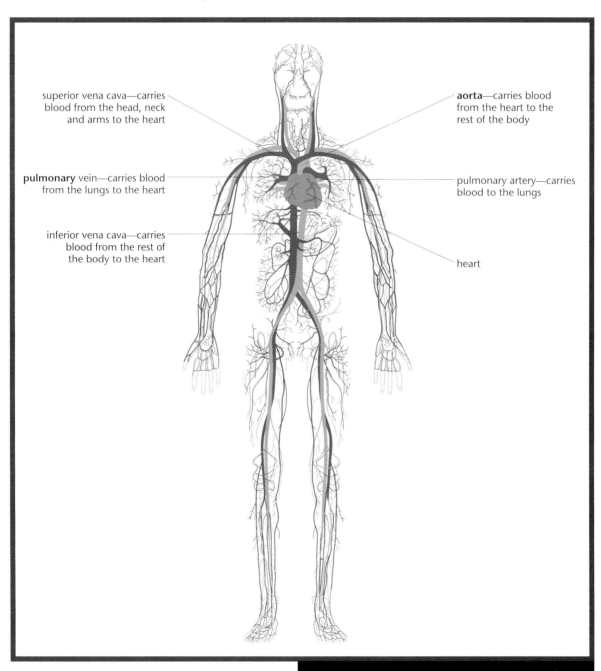

superior vena cava—carries blood from the head, neck and arms to the heart

pulmonary vein—carries blood from the lungs to the heart

inferior vena cava—carries blood from the rest of the body to the heart

aorta—carries blood from the heart to the rest of the body

pulmonary artery—carries blood to the lungs

heart

This diagram shows the position of the heart in the body and some of the major blood vessels. The arteries are shown in orange. The veins are shown in red.

Blood has three main functions:

- It transports oxygen and nutrients to tissues and removes carbon dioxide and other waste products;
- It regulates water levels and other chemicals and maintains body temperature;
- It protects against infection and disease.

To carry out these functions, blood has to travel around the body. It travels through a network of tubes called blood vessels. There are three types of blood vessels: **arteries**, which carry blood away from the heart; **veins**, which carry blood back to the heart; and **capillaries**, which link arteries and veins. These vessels carry the blood to and from every part of the body.

Blood cannot move on its own— it has to be pumped around. The heart is a very strong pump. Every time it beats, blood is pumped along the blood vessels.

This is a portrait of William Harvey, who revolutionized seventeenth-century medicine with his radical ideas about the heart and blood.

Early ideas

Until the seventeenth century, the works of Galen, an ancient Greek, formed the basis for medical thought. Galen taught that blood was produced by the liver and used by the rest of the body. An English doctor, William Harvey, proved this to be wrong. He examined hearts from different animals and studied the flow of blood in the human arm. Harvey was the first person to prove that blood circulates around the body and that the heart plays an important role in this. His textbook, *On the Motions of the Heart and Blood,* was published in 1628. It was a starting point for many other researchers.

THE HEART

An adult human heart is about the size of a small fist and has a mass of 7 to 14 ounces (200 to 400 grams). It sits almost in the center of the chest, between the two lungs, and is tipped slightly to the left. It is protected by the rib cage, the sternum (breastbone), and the spine.

A protective layer called the **pericardium** surrounds the heart. It contains a liquid called pericardial fluid that helps lubricate the heart, allowing it to move freely as it beats. Strong fibers attach the pericardium to the spine and other parts of the chest, keeping the heart firmly in place. Inside the pericardium is the heart wall. This is a thick layer of muscle with a thin covering of **membrane** on both sides. Like every other muscle in the body, the muscles of the heart need a good supply of blood to deliver oxygen and **nutrients** and take away waste products. The coronary **arteries** bring blood to the heart muscle, and the coronary **veins** carry blood away from it.

Inside the heart

The heart is made up of four spaces, called chambers. A thick wall called the septum separates the two sides of the heart. Each side has an upper chamber, or **atrium**, and a lower chamber, or **ventricle**. Blood flows into the heart by way of the atria and leaves by way of the

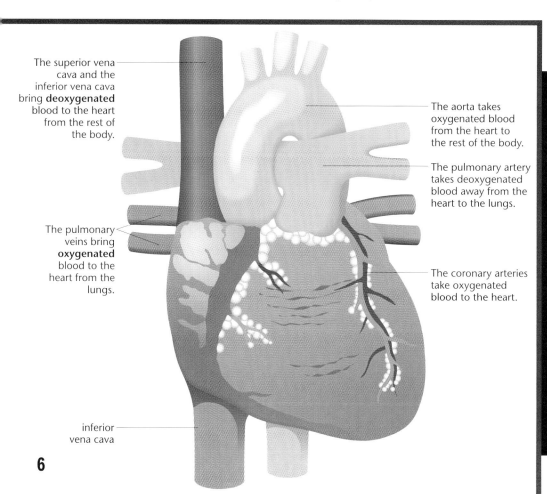

The superior vena cava and the inferior vena cava bring **deoxygenated** blood to the heart from the rest of the body.

The aorta takes oxygenated blood from the heart to the rest of the body.

The pulmonary artery takes deoxygenated blood away from the heart to the lungs.

The pulmonary veins bring **oxygenated** blood to the heart from the lungs.

The coronary arteries take oxygenated blood to the heart.

inferior vena cava

This external view of the heart shows the blood vessels that carry blood between the heart and the rest of the body. You can also see some of the coronary blood vessels that provide a blood supply for the heart muscle itself.

ventricles. The walls of the atria are thinner than those of the ventricles. This is because the atria only have to pump blood into the ventricles. The ventricles, however, have to work harder to pump blood out of the heart and into the arteries. Blood can flow through the heart in only one direction. Special flaps, called **valves,** prevent blood from flowing back in the wrong direction. When a valve relaxes, it opens a channel for blood to flow through. When the valve contracts, it blocks the channel and stops the flow of blood.

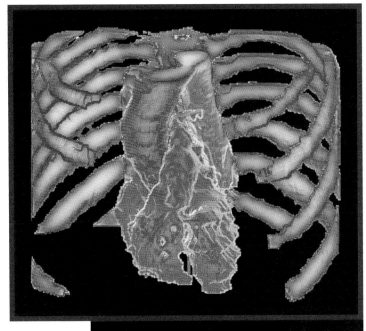

This chest scan shows a healthy human heart (orange, bottom center) inside the rib cage (pink).

Two separate loops

The heart really acts as two separate pumps, pushing blood around two separate loops. The first loop, which supplies blood to the lungs, is called the **pulmonary circulation.** The right side of the heart pumps blood along the pulmonary arteries to the lungs. In the lungs, blood loses carbon dioxide and collects oxygen. It then travels back to the left side of the heart.

The second loop, which supplies blood to the rest of the body, is called the **systemic** circulation. The left side of the heart pumps blood along the **aorta** and around every part of the body. It takes oxygen to wherever it is needed and collects and transports nutrients and waste products. It returns to the right side of the heart along two large veins, the inferior vena cava and the superior vena cava. The blood then repeats the lung loop, followed by the body loop, followed by the lung loop. . . . It's a never-ending cycle.

Heartbeat

Cardiac muscle is able to beat all the time, whether you are awake or asleep. It is called an involuntary muscle—it beats without your ever having to think about it. Under normal conditions, an adult's heart will beat approximately 70 times every minute, with each heartbeat pumping about 2.4 ounces of blood. That's more than 100,000 beats every day, or 40 million beats a year!

BLOOD VESSELS

Blood is transported around the body in a network of tubes called blood vessels. Different types of blood vessels have different structures that allow them to carry out different functions. The main types of blood vessels are **arteries**, **veins**, and **capillaries**.

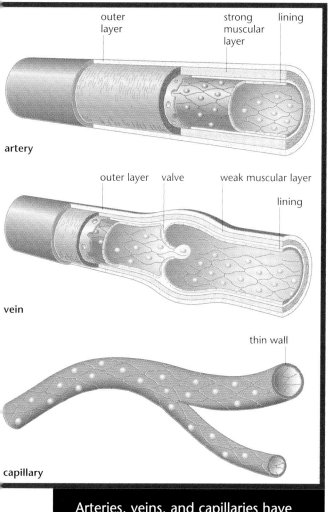

outer layer · strong muscular layer · lining

artery

outer layer · valve · weak muscular layer · lining

vein

thin wall

capillary

Arteries, veins, and capillaries have different structures that enable them to do different jobs.

Arteries

Arteries carry blood away from the heart to the rest of the body. They have very strong, thick, muscular walls that can withstand the high pressure of blood as it is pumped out of the heart. The diameter of the arteries and the thickness of their walls are greatest in the arteries nearest the heart, because these have to withstand the greatest pressure. Artery walls have three layers:
- a thick outer layer of **collagen** fibers
- a thick middle layer of elastic and muscle fibers arranged in rings
- a thin lining layer.

The walls of major arteries are very elastic, allowing them to stretch as the heart pumps blood into them. Blood flows quickly along arteries, in pulses.

Veins

Veins carry blood back to the heart. They have thinner walls than arteries, because they carry blood at a lower pressure. Their walls also have three layers:
- a thin outer layer of collagen fibers
- a thin middle layer, containing few muscle fibers
- a thin lining layer.

Blood flows slowly along veins, without a **pulse.** Veins have a system of **valves** that prevents blood from flowing backward. When blood is moving toward the heart, the valve is open. Blood pushes the flaps of the valve against the inner wall of the vein. If blood begins to flow backward, it forces the flaps of the valve down, closing the valve and preventing further backflow. Large muscles also help keep blood in the veins flowing in the right direction. For example, when you use the calf muscles in your lower leg, the muscles squeeze the veins, helping to keep the blood from flowing backwards.

Blood has to flow from the arteries into the veins, but it cannot do so directly. Arteries branch again and again, becoming narrower and narrower, eventually forming smaller vessels called **arterioles**. Arterioles branch many more times into the tiniest blood vessels, called capillaries.

Capillaries

Capillaries are tiny, narrow vessels that occur in branching networks throughout body tissues. Only a few special tissues, such as the cornea and lens of the eye, do not have a capillary network. Capillary walls are made up of just a single layer of cells. Gases, **nutrients,** and wastes can easily pass from the blood through the capillaries and into tissues, and from tissues into the blood by a process called diffusion. This means that particles of a gas or liquid move from an area of high concentration to an area of lower concentration, thus creating a balance.

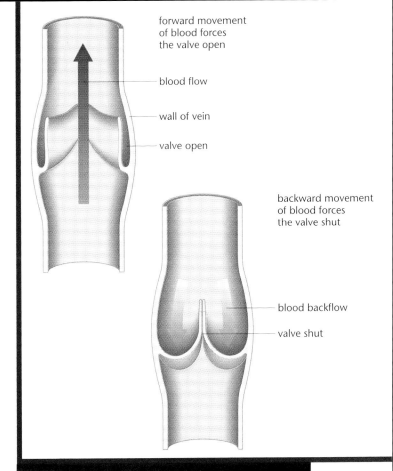

forward movement of blood forces the valve open

blood flow

wall of vein

valve open

backward movement of blood forces the valve shut

blood backflow

valve shut

These diagrams show how valves in veins prevent blood from flowing backward. Blood flowing in the right direction pushes the flaps of the valves flat against the wall of the vein. If blood starts to flow backward, the flaps are pushed down, shutting the valve.

Capillaries unite, forming larger vessels called venules. Venules unite, forming small veins and eventually large veins.

Exercise

Exercise helps to maintain a healthy **circulation.** The more exercise you do, the faster your heart pumps, and the greater the volume of blood is pumped. Arteries and veins have to cope with this extra workload and so become stronger and healthier. The heart muscle itself becomes stronger and larger with exercise. A trained athlete's heart can pump more blood, with fewer heartbeats, than the heart of a person who does little exercise. The resting heart rate for an average adult is usually around 70 beats per minute, while that of a trained athlete may be as low as 40 to 60 beats per minute.

If you lay your fingers gently on the inside of your wrist, you will feel a gentle, regular beating—your **pulse.** Every time your heart beats, blood is forced along the **arteries,** creating the pulse you feel. Counting the number of beats in one minute will tell you how quickly your heart is beating. Medical professionals use a stethoscope to listen to the actual sounds made by the heart as it beats.

The **atria** and **ventricles** take turns relaxing and contracting. The contraction phase is called systole, and the relaxation phase is called diastole. During a normal heartbeat, the two atria contract—this is called atrial systole. Meanwhile, the two ventricles relax—this is called ventricular diastole. This is followed by the ventricles contracting (ventricular systole) while the atria relax (atrial diastole).

The stages of a heartbeat

The sounds of a heartbeat are made by the **valves** as they shut to control the flow of blood. When you feel your pulse, you feel a single surge of blood. But each heartbeat is made up of two separate sounds, one after the other. This is often written as "lub dub . . . lub dub . . . lub dub. . . ."

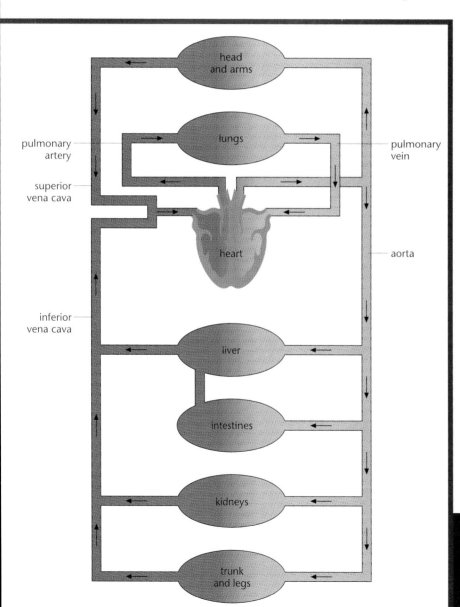

pulmonary artery
pulmonary vein
superior vena cava
heart
aorta
inferior vena cava
head and arms
lungs
liver
intestines
kidneys
trunk and legs

This diagram shows the circulation of the blood to the lungs and to the rest of the body.

Each heartbeat has three stages:
1. With the valves between the atria and ventricles shut, the atria relax. The right atrium fills with blood from the body, and the left atrium fills with blood from the lungs.
2. The blood in the atria pushes against the valves, forcing them open. The atria contract, and the ventricles relax. Blood flows out of the atria and into the ventricles.
3. When the ventricles are full, the pressure of the blood forces the flaps of the lower

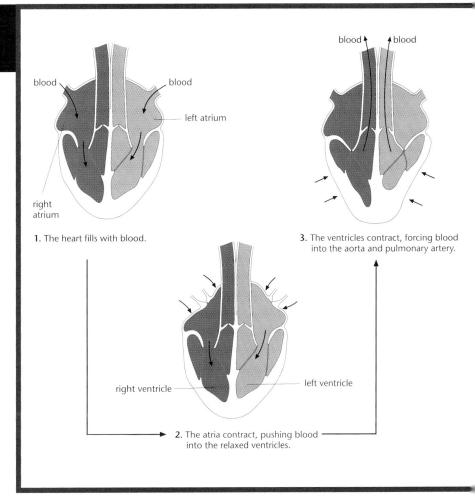

blood   blood

left atrium

right
atrium

1. The heart fills with blood.

blood ↑   ↑ blood

3. The ventricles contract, forcing blood into the aorta and pulmonary artery.

right ventricle   left ventricle

2. The atria contract, pushing blood into the relaxed ventricles.

valves upward, and the valves snap shut. As they shut, they make the first "lub" sound of the heartbeat. The ventricles then contract, pushing the blood upward. The upper valves relax and open, allowing blood to flow out of the ventricles and into the **pulmonary** artery and **aorta**. With the ventricles empty, the upper valves snap shut, creating the second "dub" sound of the heartbeat. Then another heartbeat begins, going back to stage 1.

Upper and lower valves

The upper and lower valves of the heart operate like gates, forced open and shut by blood pushing against them. The upper valves control blood flow from the atria into the ventricles. They are larger than the lower valves and are anchored to the heart wall by strong tendons. As the valves shut, muscles attached to the base of each valve contract to keep them from being turned inside out. The lower valves control blood flow out of the ventricles. They are smaller than the upper valves. Each valve has three flaps attached directly to the heart wall.

The heart affects every aspect of our lives. It must work efficiently if we are to stay fit and healthy. So it makes sense to take good care of it! Lifestyle—what we do and how we live—has a big effect on our heart and **circulation.** You can do a lot to keep your heart healthy by getting plenty of exercise and eating the right kinds of foods. You should also avoid things such as drinking too much alcohol, smoking cigarettes, and taking other drugs.

Aerobic exercise, such as swimming, helps keep the heart healthy and strong.

Exercise

Exercise is very important. The heart is a muscle and—like any other muscle—the more it is used, the stronger it becomes. Some types of exercise make the heart work harder than others.

Aerobic exercise

Aerobic exercises include activities such as swimming, cycling, and running. They all use the large muscles of the body, making big movements, and this increases the amount of oxygen the body needs. To get extra oxygen to the muscles, the heart has to pump blood around the body more quickly. This makes it stronger and increases the amount of blood that it can pump. These activities can also help lower blood pressure and keep body weight down. Over a period of time, they can also increase the mass of the heart, making it stronger. Most doctors recommend three to five twenty-minute aerobic sessions each week. This should keep the heart and circulatory system at peak fitness.

Anaerobic exercise

Anaerobic exercise, such as weightlifting or yoga, is good for building body strength and suppleness. However, because the large body muscles are not repeatedly contracting and relaxing quickly, they are not using much extra oxygen, and so the heart does not do much extra work. For overall fitness, it is a good idea to combine the two types of exercise.

Nutrition

The food we eat is important in keeping our heart and circulatory system in first-class condition. Your body needs a variety of **nutrients**, so you should try to eat a balanced diet containing meat, fish, eggs, or nuts (good sources of **protein**); fruit and vegetables (good sources of **vitamins** and **minerals**); starchy foods (for **carbohydrates**); and dairy products (for proteins and fats). You do need some fats for energy and to provide the chemicals your body needs to maintain its tissues. But there is a strong link between eating a lot of fatty foods and developing heart disease. Fat can lead to clogging of blood vessels, increasing the chance of heart attack or **stroke**. It can also cause weight gain, and this puts an extra strain on the heart. Some types of fat are better for us than others. Good sources of "healthy fats" include oily fish, such as salmon and sardines, and olive oil.

Polluting the body

Polluting the body with alcohol, cigarettes, and other drugs is not a very healthy thing to do. All of these have a bad effect on the heart.

- Alcohol can lead to high blood pressure and damage to the heart muscle. It also leads to weight gain, making the heart work harder.
- Cigarettes increase the risk of **blood clots** that can cause strokes and heart attacks. Small blood vessels may become narrower, so the heart is under strain as it works harder to push the blood through.
- Other drugs can have a wide variety of effects on the body. Some, such as cocaine, may have a direct effect on the heart and blood and can cause other serious damage to the body. It is best to avoid these drugs completely. Other drugs, such as caffeine, may have smaller, less serious effects, but it makes sense to limit the amounts you use.

The heart needs a constant supply of blood in order to function and stay healthy. This is provided by the coronary **arteries**. If blood flow through these arteries is reduced for any reason, the heart muscle becomes short of oxygen and begins to die—otherwise known as a heart attack.

Causes

The most common cause of a heart attack is blockage of the coronary arteries by a buildup of fatty deposits or by a **blood clot**. This is especially likely in people who have eaten a diet high in fat for many years. A fatty substance can collect on the inside of the artery walls. As more and more builds up, the patches of this fatty substance get bigger and bigger. They begin to make the artery narrower, restricting the flow of blood. This can lead to a chest pain called angina.

A blood clot may start to form around these patches of fat. When the blood clot completely blocks a coronary artery, the part of the heart muscle supplied by that artery is starved of blood and dies. This is a severe heart attack.

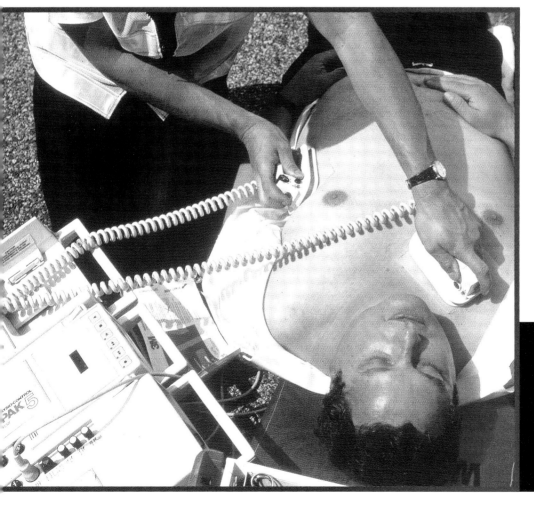

Medical teams can carry out emergency treatment to improve the chances of survival after a heart attack.

Avoiding a heart attack

After suffering a heart attack, many patients are advised to alter their lifestyle. Heart attacks are much more common in people who:

- smoke
- eat a lot of fatty foods
- are overweight
- get little exercise
- suffer a lot of stress.

Patients who have had a heart attack are encouraged to change these habits. It makes sense for everyone to avoid these things if possible.

Heart attacks can sometimes occur in people who get plenty of exercise, eat a healthy diet, and do not smoke cigarettes. Some people just have higher than normal levels of **cholesterol** in their blood, making blocking of arteries more likely. Other diseases, such as diabetes, can also increase the risk of heart attack. There may be **genetic** links, too, as some families do seem to be more at risk of heart disease than others.

Symptoms

The main symptom of a heart attack is serious chest pain, often accompanied by pain or tingling in the left arm. A patient may also sweat, feel sick, and find it hard to breathe.

It is important to get medical help for a heart attack patient as quickly as possible. The medical team can assess the situation and give the patient drugs to relieve pain. If the patient is unconscious, has stopped breathing, and has no **pulse**, the team may give **cardiopulmonary resuscitation (CPR)** to try to maintain an oxygen supply and keep the blood **circulating**. The heart muscle may simply twitch, or fibrillate, instead of contract properly. The team may use defibrillation equipment to give an electric shock to stimulate the heart to begin beating again. Drugs can be used to dissolve a clot and to reduce the chances of another clot forming.

Treatment

A patient who has suffered a heart attack is likely to spend some time in the hospital, where he or she can rest and be monitored. Some patients may need an operation to reroute some blood vessels to improve the blood supply to the heart. When their doctors feel that they are well enough, patients need to slowly build their level of activity again. A range of drugs, including aspirin, may be needed for a long time after a heart attack to reduce the risk of future heart attacks.

HEART MONITORING

For many patients, counting the **pulse** is a routine procedure. For patients with heart problems, monitoring and investigating the heartbeat can help the medical staff assess how well the heart is functioning and decide on the best form of treatment.

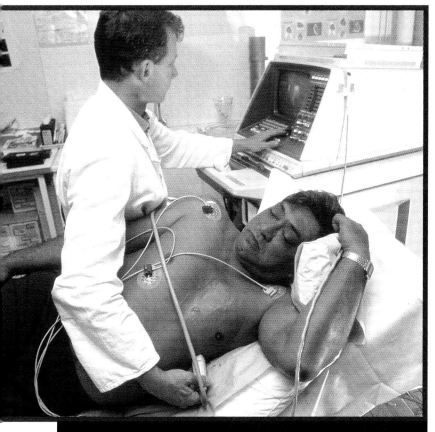

This patient's heart function is being investigated using an ultrasound echocardiogram.

Listening to the heart

Using a stethoscope, a doctor can listen to the sounds made by the heart as the **valves** open and shut and blood flows through. Unusual rushing or gurgling noises may indicate that one or more valves are not working properly, and the doctor may decide to send the patient for further tests. Conditions such as heart murmurs may be monitored regularly to check that the heart function is stable.

Ultrasound echocardiogram

Heart function can be monitored using an ultrasound echocardiogram. This machine sends high-frequency sound waves through the chest. The waves bounce off the heart and are converted into electrical signals that can be displayed on a monitor. The doctor can then see all four chambers of the heart and the valves. Echocardiograms can be used to detect **blood clots**, faulty valves, tumors, and other problems.

Electrocardiograph

Another method for investigating the heart is to use an electrocardiograph (ECG or EKG). As the heart beats, the muscle creates electrical changes. Electrodes that can detect these changes are attached to the patient's chest, arms, and legs, and the results are displayed on a monitor or a printout. Information from an ECG can confirm whether or not a patient has suffered a heart attack. It can also be used to detect whether or not any areas of the heart are damaged.

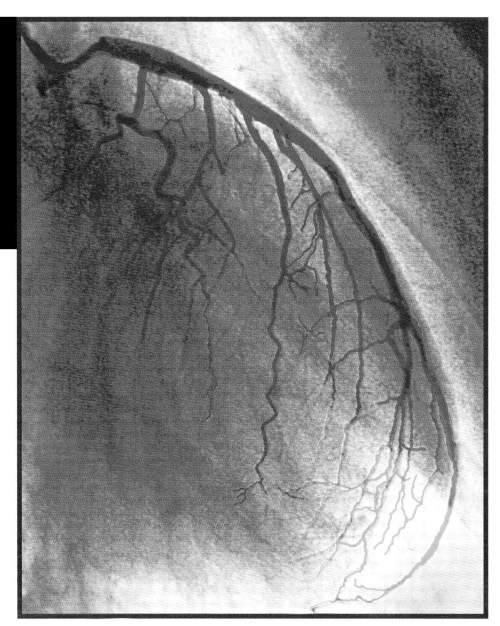

If a radioactive chemical is injected into the bloodstream, it will be carried to every part of the body. Using a special camera that detects radioactivity, a nuclear scanner can create a color-coded picture of the heart as it beats. This can show the blood passing through the heart, dead or damaged heart muscle, and areas of the heart that are short of oxygen.

Angiocardiography

Angiocardiography is another way to look inside the heart. A hollow, flexible tube is inserted into a **vein** in the thigh, arm, or neck and moved slowly until it reaches the heart. Dyes can be injected by way of the tube and then detected by a special camera and displayed on a monitor.

In adults, surgery can improve heart function and reduce the risk of future heart attacks. Some babies are born with heart **defects**, and these may need immediate surgery to keep the baby alive. Other less serious conditions can be corrected when the child is a little older. Surgical techniques are improving and advancing all the time. One of the greatest breakthroughs in heart surgery was the invention of the heart-lung machine.

Heart-lung machine

It is very difficult to operate on a heart that is beating and full of blood. Ideally, the heart should be still and empty, but blood must collect oxygen and circulate to all parts of the body if the patient is to survive. In 1953 the first heart-lung machine was introduced. It worked just like the lungs do. Blood flowed from the vena cava, through a pump, and to an oxygenator. Here, carbon dioxide was removed and oxygen, which is needed by all the body organs and tissues, was added. The blood then passed through a filter and was pumped back into the **aorta** and around the rest of the body. For the first time a patient could be kept alive without his or her own heart working. Heart surgeons could now attempt more complex surgeries than ever before.

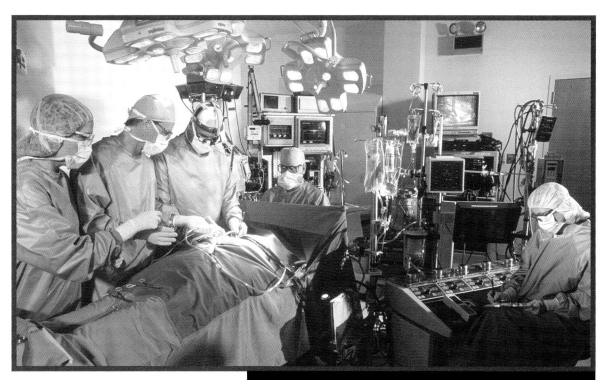

The heart-lung machine takes over the function of the heart and lungs during heart surgery. Blood is pumped from the vena cava, through the oxygenator and filter, then back to the body.

Heart-lung machines have been refined and developed since the first one was introduced. The patient's body is often cooled so that there is no heart movement at all. The very newest methods allow doctors to cool just the heart and not the rest of the body.

Coronary artery bypass

In patients who have narrowed, blocked, or damaged coronary **arteries**, the blood supply to the heart is restricted and the heart is unable to function properly. This means that the patient is less and less able to carry on with normal everyday activities. Even small tasks can cause breathlessness and the severe pain of angina. An operation to bypass a section of the coronary artery, called a coronary artery bypass, may help such patients. A blood vessel is taken from another part of the body and **grafted** to a coronary artery, on either side of the blockage. The blood can then flow along the new vessel, bypassing the blockage. The blood supply to the heart muscle is improved, allowing the patient greater mobility and levels of activity than before.

Angioplasty

If coronary arteries are blocked, the blood supply to the heart muscle becomes reduced. Angioplasty is a method to unblock the coronary arteries. A plastic tube is put into an artery, often in the groin, and guided to the coronary vessels. Dye inserted into the tube is carried to the coronary vessels, and blockages can be seen on angiograms, or X-rays of blood vessels. A tiny air-filled balloon can then be inserted, by way of the tube, to squash the blockage back against the blood vessel wall. This allows blood to flow again. A coil of stainless steel, called a stent, can also be inserted to hold the vessel open permanently.

Heart surgery in babies

Most babies are born with normal, healthy hearts. But some have defects that require heart surgery. If a baby is born with a hole in the wall between the two sides of the heart, blood can move freely from one side of the heart to the other. This means that the **oxygenated** blood does not get pumped properly to the rest of the body. A surgeon can close the hole either by stitching it or by putting a plastic patch over it. Blood can then circulate normally, and the baby will be fit and healthy.

Blood vessels that carry blood to and from the heart may be incorrectly connected to the heart or may be narrow or badly formed. There are surgical procedures to connect the heart and vessels correctly, mend the vessels, and widen narrow vessels to improve blood flow.

PACEMAKERS

The heart must beat regularly for blood to be **circulated** efficiently around the body. Normally the heart is stimulated to do this by its own pacemaker. The heart's natural pacemaker is the sinoatrial node (SA node), a small, specialized area of the right **atrium**. When the body is resting, the SA node generates an electrical signal about 70 times every minute. This stimulates the heart muscle, making the atria and then the **ventricles** contract, pumping blood out of the heart. If the SA node does not function properly, an artificial pacemaker can be implanted to help regulate the heartbeat.

Arrhythmia

A normal heartbeat can be disrupted if the SA node develops an abnormal rhythm or rate, if the normal pathway for the electrical signal is interrupted, or if another part of the heart takes over as pacemaker. The electrical signals may be erratic: too fast, too slow, or too irregular.

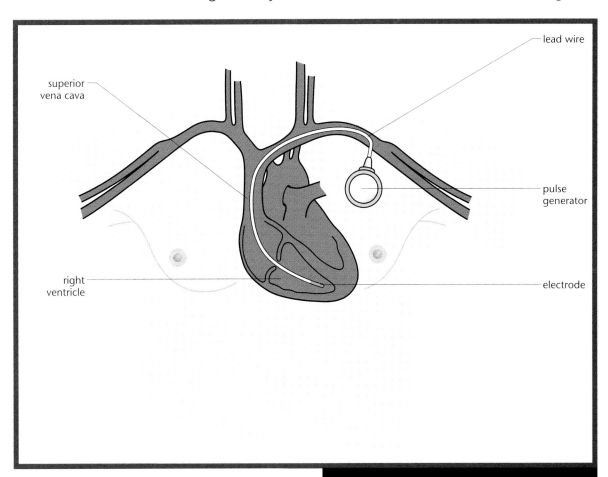

A pacemaker is implanted under the skin, close to the collarbone.

The erratic heartbeat that results is called an arrhythmia. An arrhythmia can mean that the body is not receiving enough blood. The patient may feel weak, tired, dizzy, and faint; the blood pressure may drop; and he or she may feel heart palpitations—rapid or irregular heartbeats.

Artificial pacemakers

Artificial pacemakers take over the task of regulating the heartbeat. Arrhythmias can affect people of all ages—tiny babies, young children, teenagers, and adults. And artificial pacemakers can be used for any patient, no matter the age. There are several different types of devices that can do this, but they all work on the same basic principles.

A permanent pacemaker is implanted under the skin, usually just below the collarbone. Some simply send electrical signals to start or regulate a slow heartbeat. Others can also monitor the heartbeat and send signals only if it becomes slow or irregular. Some modern pacemakers can also adjust the rate of the heartbeat, increasing it when the patient is engaged in physical activity. Pacemakers can send signals to a single chamber of the heart. More sophisticated pacemakers are used if two chambers need to be regulated. There are a variety of different designs of pacemakers, all of which have slightly different shapes and sizes.

Battery power

Pacemakers run on a special battery that generates timed electrical signals. Like all batteries, the battery of a pacemaker does not last forever, so while it usually lasts a few years, it does need to be replaced eventually. This can be done under **local anesthetic.** Pacemakers also need to be checked regularly to ensure they are working properly and to check the batteries. Modern pacemakers can be tested and adjusted painlessly from outside the body with a radiowave programmer.

Living with a pacemaker
A pacemaker can help a patient with an arrhythmia lead a normal, active life. He or she can do things such as drive, swim, play sports, and other activities. Most medicines do not affect pacemakers and neither do electrical tools and devices such as televisions and microwaves. However, pacemakers can trigger security devices at airports! This can be embarrassing for the patient but will not damage the pacemaker or keep it from working properly.

The four **valves** of the heart control the flow of blood. If these are damaged or do not function properly, blood may not be pumped efficiently to the rest of the body. Babies may be born with faulty valves, or valves may be damaged by diseases such as rheumatic fever, or **bacterial infections**. Aging and normal wear and tear may weaken or stiffen heart valves. To restore efficient blood **circulation,** faulty valves may require surgical repair or replacement.

Heart murmur

Heart valve **defects** can often be detected using a stethoscope. The normal "lub dub" sounds of the heartbeat may be hidden by the sounds of blood rushing through the heart. This is called a heart murmur, and it usually indicates a valve disorder. A heart murmur may be caused by:

- a backflow of blood through a valve that does not close properly. The heart works less efficiently because it has to pump some blood twice. The heart chambers may also be enlarged because they have to hold more blood.
- restricted blood flow due to a valve that does not open properly. Blood pressure in the heart increases because blood builds up behind the faulty valve. The heart has to work harder to pump the higher-pressure blood.

If the damage to a valve is not too severe, a surgeon may be able to repair it. Stretched tissue can be removed, and the edges may be stitched together. However, most heart murmers are harmless.

Using animal valves

There is a lot of debate about whether or not it is right to use animals to cure human health problems. Some people argue that it is perfectly justifiable to kill a pig and remove the heart valves if this will save a person's life and allow them to live normally and be active. Other people argue that we should respect animals and that we have no right to use them in this way. What do you think? Would you want to have a pig's valve if you were ill? Or would you risk dying rather than hurt an animal? The debate will go on and on. . . .

Replacement valves

A valve that is seriously damaged may need to be replaced with a new one. Several types of valves are available, including the following:

- valves from human donors. Valves from a donated human heart are frozen in liquid nitrogen until the day before the operation. Very delicate surgery is needed to ensure that the donor valves fit the patient's heart exactly.
- valves made from human tissue. A new valve can be constructed using tissue, such as part of the vena cava, from the patient's own body. The tissue is attached to a stainless steel frame to strengthen it and is then inserted into the heart.
- valves from animals. Valves from pigs' hearts can be successfully inserted into human hearts. Tissue from cows' hearts can also be used to make replacement valves for human hearts.
- artificial valves. A lot of research has been carried out to design and produce an artificial heart valve. The first, made in 1952, was a ball valve. The ball was pushed up, opening the valve, when blood was pumped out of the heart chamber. When blood flowed backward, it pushed the ball back into place, closing the valve. Single disk valves were introduced in 1965, and the design was refined and improved to produce the first bileaflet valve in 1977. These have two disks and a hinge and have proved to be very successful. Patients are living longer and are having fewer complications than with the original ball valves.

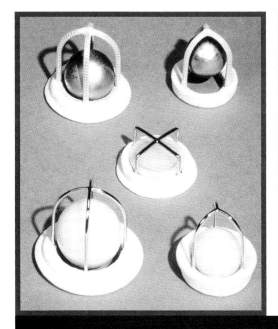

A selection of ball valves (left). As blood is pumped out of the heart chamber, it lifts the ball; backflow of blood pushes the ball back into place. A modern bileaflet valve (right) has two disks and a hinge.

HEART TRANSPLANT

For some patients, heart disease may be too serious for surgical repair. For many years doctors could do little to help, and the patients would eventually die. The first successful human heart transplant offered a way of treating these patients, giving them another chance at life.

Rejection

The main problem that early heart transplant patients faced was rejection. Their **immune system** recognized the donor heart as "foreign" and attacked it in the same way it would attack an infection. Drugs were developed to suppress the immune system and overcome the rejection problem. Although these were largely successful, they led to an increased risk of infection and other illnesses. Without an active immune system, infections that are normally relatively minor can rapidly become very serious.

Stages of a transplant

There are five main stages of a heart transplant:
Finding a suitable donor: Tissue typing tries to match the donor's cells as closely as possible to the patient's. This reduces the risk of rejection.
Transporting the donor heart: The donor and patient are rarely at the same hospital, and the operation has to take place as soon as possible after the donor's death. The donor heart is packed into sterile bags, stored at 39°F (4°C), and transported by airplane or helicopter. Land transport usually has a police escort to ensure maximum speed.
Preparation for surgery: While the donor heart is being transported, the operation on the patient begins. The chest is opened, and everything is prepared for the new heart to arrive.
The transplant: The patient's blood **circulation** is maintained by a heart-lung machine. The new heart is put into place, and the blood vessels are connected. It usually begins to beat right away.
After the transplant: The patient is usually conscious within a few hours. He or she takes immunosuppressive drugs to prevent rejection of the new heart, and strict precautions are followed to prevent infection.

Dr. Christiaan Barnard, the surgeon who performed the first heart transplant, is on the left in this picture.

The first transplants

For many years doctors had been experimenting with transplanting tissues and organs. The first successful human heart transplant was carried out on December 3, 1967, by Dr. Christiaan Barnard in Cape Town, South Africa. The patient was Louis Washkansky, a 55-year-old grocer. The heart he received came from a 24-year-old woman who had been killed in a car crash.

Louis Washkansky lived for only eighteen days after his transplant operation. While this may not seem very long, it was enough to prove to doctors around the world that transplants could be done successfully. In January 1968 a second transplant was performed. The patient, Philip Blaiberg, lived for 563 days afterward.

Artificial hearts

Because heart transplants are very expensive, and there is a shortage of donor hearts, operations are performed only on patients who are very seriously ill with severe heart disease. Without a transplant, these patients would die. Researchers have worked for years to design an artificial heart, but it has proven to be difficult to produce one that is reliable and safe. A major advance was made in July 2001 when an artificial heart was successfully implanted into a patient, Robert Tools. He lived for five months afterward. The device, which weighs about 2 pounds (900 grams), is made of titanium and a special plastic. It has an internal battery that lasts about half an hour. An external battery pack has to be worn at all other times to keep the device pumping blood. This is a positive and encouraging breakthrough, and an identical device has been implanted into six other patients. One, Thomas Christerson, is still alive one year after his operation. If they are found to be successful in the long term, these artificial hearts could benefit many patients suffering from heart disease.

Louis Washkansky is seen here sitting up in bed after having the first successful heart transplant.

PROBLEMS WITH ARTERIES

Arteries are the vessels that carry blood, rich in oxygen, to all parts of the body. If they become blocked or damaged, the blood supply is interrupted, causing a variety of problems.

Atherosclerosis

Atherosclerosis occurs when fat, **fibrin**, and other debris collect on the inside of an artery wall. Eating a lot of fatty foods, smoking cigarettes, and being very overweight can all increase the risk of atherosclerosis. The lining of a healthy artery is pale and smooth. An unhealthy artery has yellow streaks and a rough surface. Thick, white fibers form, making irregular bumps that restrict blood flow. As the blood flows over these lumps, some blood cells stick to the rough surface, and a **blood clot**, or thrombus, may form.

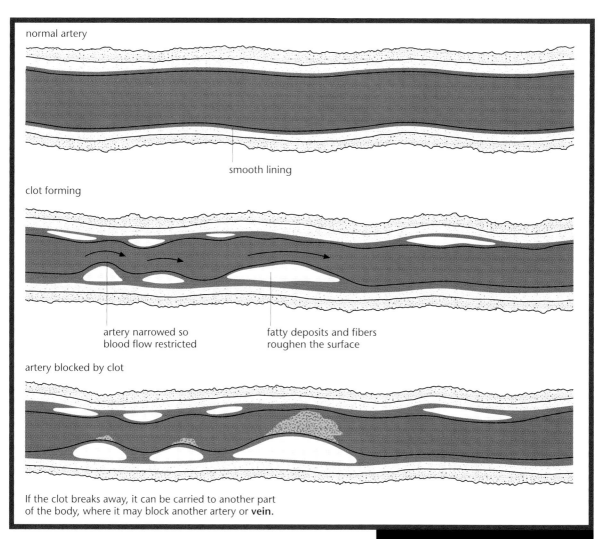

normal artery

smooth lining

clot forming

artery narrowed so
blood flow restricted

fatty deposits and fibers
roughen the surface

artery blocked by clot

If the clot breaks away, it can be carried to another part
of the body, where it may block another artery or **vein**.

These diagrams show how
a clot can form in an artery.

Thrombosis

A blood clot may block an artery, stopping blood flow. This is called a thrombosis. If a blood clot blocks a coronary artery, a heart attack may occur. If it blocks an artery supplying blood to the brain, the patient may suffer a **stroke.** The brain needs a continuous supply of oxygen, and if this is interrupted for even a short time, there may be temporary or permanent brain damage—it may even be fatal. An angiogram can show exactly where the blockage is, and drugs may be injected to dissolve the clot.

Embolism

If a blood clot breaks free from the damaged artery, it may travel around the body in the bloodstream and cause a blockage, or **embolism,** in an artery somewhere else. Blocked arteries can sometimes be cleared by injection of a drug to dissolve the blood clot. If an embolism blocks an artery that carries blood to the brain, the patient may suffer a stroke.

Aneurysm

Atherosclerosis can weaken an artery wall, causing a section of it to stretch and bulge like a balloon. This is called an aneurysm. Although the bulge itself may not cause a problem, because it is weakened it may burst at any time. This causes internal bleeding, or a hemorrhage, and the patient is likely to suffer severe pain and shock. If the aneurysm is in an artery supplying blood to the brain, it may cause a stroke.

Raynaud's disease

Capillaries in the skin can help regulate body temperature. When the body gets hot, **arterioles** force more blood into the capillaries. As the blood passes close to the surface of the skin, it loses heat and the body cools down. When the body gets cold, arterioles restrict the amount of blood flowing into the capillaries. Less blood flows to the surface of the skin, and heat is conserved. Raynaud's disease causes the arterioles in the fingers and toes to constrict, reducing the blood supply to capillaries, sometimes for just a few minutes, sometimes for much longer. The fingers and toes turn white and cold. When the arterioles relax, blood rushes back into the capillaries, causing intense pain and tingling.

Raynaud's disease is much worse in cold weather, when the tiny blood capillaries constrict and almost completely stop blood flow to the affected areas. People with Raynaud's disease try to avoid the pain by keeping their hands and feet wrapped well in warm gloves and socks.

Veins carry **deoxygenated** blood back to the heart. As it travels around the body, the blood collects waste products, such as carbon dioxide produced by the organs and tissues. Any problems with veins may lead to reduced efficiency of blood **circulation**, causing problems in other organs and tissues.

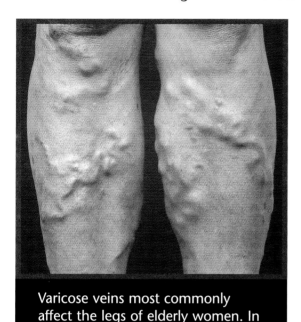

Varicose veins most commonly affect the legs of elderly women. In severe cases, like this, surgery might be needed.

Varicose veins

Varicose veins occur most often in the legs. If the **valves** become weak, blood flows backward and collects in pools. This stretches the veins, and eventually they become permanently stretched and twisted. They may be seen as dark, knotty threads under the skin.

Often, varicose veins cause little problem and no treatment is needed. Mild symptoms can include swelling in the lower legs, pain, and cramps, which can often be eased by wearing elastic stockings that squeeze inward on the leg, preventing swelling. More serious cases can be treated by injections of drugs. Others may need surgery.

Varicose veins may be caused by a **hereditary** valve weakness but can be made worse by pregnancy, lack of exercise, and smoking. People whose jobs require them to stand for a long periods often develop varicose veins.

Phlebitis

Phlebitis is inflammation of a vein, usually the result of an injury or infection. It occurs most often in the veins of the legs. The area may be swollen, the leg may feel heavy and uncomfortable, and a red streak may appear along the line of the vein.

Phlebitis is usually treated by resting with the legs raised, painkillers, and **antibiotics** if there is an infection. Elastic stockings and bandages may help to reduce the swelling.

Deep Vein Thrombosis (DVT)

When a **blood clot**, or thrombus, develops in a deep vein, usually in the thigh or calf, the blood flow through the vein is restricted or

Blood is not flowing properly through the veins of this leg, causing the skin to be discolored and flaky.

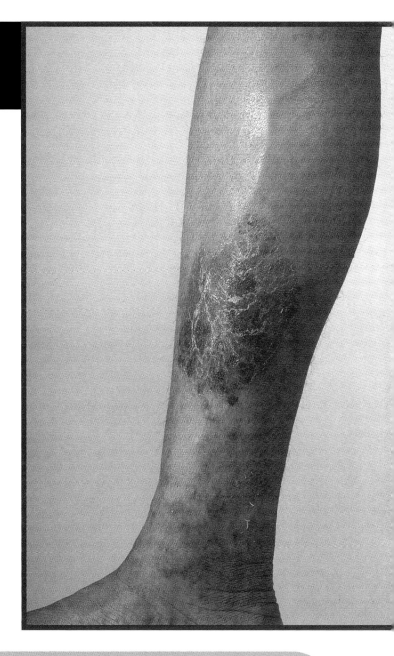

stopped completely. DVT can be caused by poor circulation, heart disease, severe varicose veins, or lack of exercise.

DVT can cause tenderness or a sharp pain in the leg, fever, and a rapid heartbeat. If a clot breaks free, it can travel to other parts of the body, most commonly the lungs. If it blocks an **artery** in the lungs, it can cause a **pulmonary embolism**, which can be fatal. Tests for DVT include an ultrasound scan, X-rays of the veins after injection of dye, and tests to determine how quickly the blood clots. Treatment usually includes anticoagulant drugs that make the blood less "sticky" and therefore prevent more clots. Patients can also help prevent clots by avoiding socks that restrict blood flow, resting with their feet raised, wearing elastic stockings, and keeping their toes and ankles moving regularly.

Economy class syndrome

DVT has been found to occur more frequently in people who have taken long airline flights. It is thought that because they have little legroom, passengers do not move around enough to keep blood flowing efficiently. This is often referred to as "economy class syndrome," because space is more restricted in cheaper airline seats, making it harder to move around. Although it can affect anybody, people most likely to suffer DVT during a flight are those who are overweight, pregnant, elderly, smokers, or already suffering from heart disease. Doctors suggest that you can reduce the risk of DVT during a flight by wiggling your toes and bending your ankles regularly and by walking up and down the aisle at least once an hour.

When the **ventricles** of the heart contract, blood is pumped into the **arteries**. The force with which the blood is pushed against the walls of the arteries is called blood pressure. Doctors measure blood pressure using a sphygmomanometer and a stethoscope. High blood pressure can increase the risk of some other illnesses.

Blood pressure depends on four things:
- the volume of blood in the arteries
- the elasticity of the artery walls
- the rate at which the ventricles contract
- the force with which the ventricles contract.

Systolic pressure is the highest pressure inside the arteries. It occurs when the ventricles contract. Diastolic pressure is the lowest pressure inside the arteries. It occurs when the ventricles are relaxed, just before they contract again.

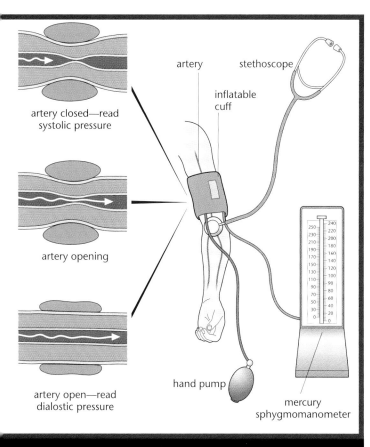

artery closed—read systolic pressure

artery opening

artery open—read dialostic pressure

artery

stethoscope

inflatable cuff

hand pump

mercury sphygmomanometer

In this diagram, you can see what happens when blood pressure is measured. Pressure from the cuff completely closes the artery in the top diagram. The artery is partially open in the middle diagram and fully open in the bottom one.

Measuring blood pressure

A cuff is wrapped around the patient's arm and inflated as the doctor squeezes a rubber bulb. As the cuff is inflated, it squeezes the arm and squashes the main artery on the inside of the arm shut, cutting off the blood flow. The doctor places the stethoscope over the route of the artery and listens. When the pressure is just above systolic pressure, the artery is closed completely, and there will be no sound through the stethoscope. The doctor reads the pressure off the scale of the sphygmomanometer. The cuff is then allowed to deflate slowly, and as the artery begins to open, the doctor hears the sound of blood rushing through the artery. The sound gets louder and then quieter again as the blood flow returns to normal. When the sound stops completely, blood is flowing normally and the doctor reads the diastolic pressure from the scale.

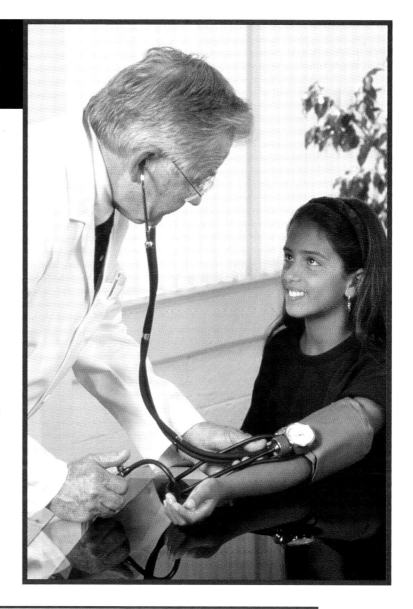

Blood pressure is measured in millimeters of mercury (mmHg)—the amount of pressure needed to raise the mercury in the sphygmomanometer scale. A normal, healthy young adult would expect to have a systolic pressure of 120mmHg and a diastolic pressure of 80mmHg. This is written as 120/80mmHg.

Blood pressure changes with age. A newborn baby's blood pressure is very low, and it gradually increases during the first few months of life. As we age, blood pressure often increases. It is considered to be high if it is greater than 140/90 mmHg.

Hypertension

High blood pressure is also called hypertension. In a person with hypertension, the arterial walls may be hard and thick and less elastic than usual, making the heart work harder to pump blood.

There are usually no symptoms of high blood pressure, and it is often detected only when a patient goes to a doctor with some unrelated problem. It becomes more common as people get older and is linked to obesity, stress, a high-fat diet, smoking, and lack of exercise. Drugs can often be prescribed to reduce blood pressure, but the best treatment is a change of lifestyle— losing weight, improving the diet, giving up smoking, and increasing exercise.

Blood is a liquid containing millions of red blood cells, which make it look red. It also contains millions of white blood cells. Blood has three main functions: transportation, regulation, and protection. It transports oxygen and carbon dioxide, **nutrients** and waste products, **hormones,** drugs, and heat. Blood helps regulate pH levels, preventing body fluids from becoming too acidic or too alkaline. It also helps regulate body temperature and the water content of tissues. Blood clots to prevent excess blood loss after injury, and it also provides defense against infection and disease.

Temperature control

The blood maintains the body's temperature. The temperature of the blood is raised as it passes through the liver and muscles. As the blood flows through the body the heat is carried to all tissues. To lose heat, **capillaries** in the skin dilate, or relax, allowing more blood to flow through and therefore increasing heat loss. To retain heat, blood capillaries in the skin constrict, or become narrow, reducing the amount of blood that flows through and therefore reducing heat loss.

Plasma

The liquid part of blood is called **plasma.** It is about 92 percent water and 8 percent **solutes,** which are mainly plasma **proteins.** All nutrients, waste products, hormones, and drugs dissolve in the plasma and are transported around the body. Water is also transported as part of the plasma. Water moves between body tissues and blood plasma by osmosis, a process similar to diffusion, to maintain the water content of body tissues and fluids.

Red blood cells

Red blood cells, also called erythrocytes, are extremely tiny disk-shaped cells with concave top and bottom surfaces. Their size and shape allow them to squeeze through narrow capillaries without being damaged. They are simple fluid-filled sacs, each containing about 280 million **molecules** of hemoglobin, the **protein** that gives blood its red color and carries oxygen. Red blood cells are made in **bone marrow** and live for about 120 days. At the end of this time, they become fragile and begin to lose their shape. They are then broken down by the **spleen** and the liver.

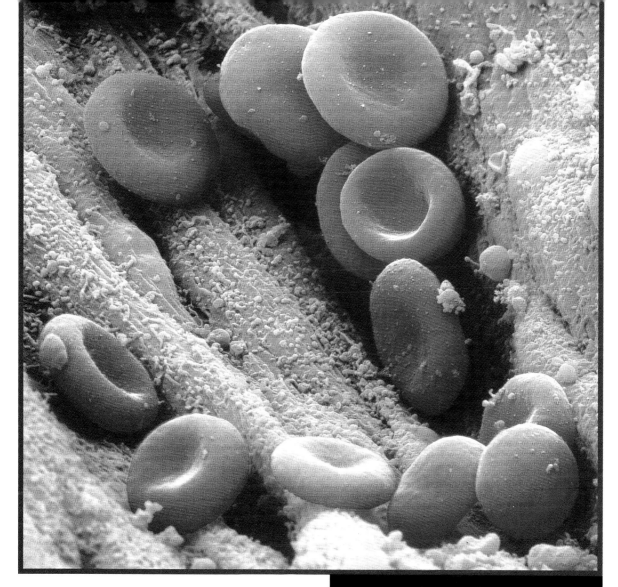

White blood cells

White blood cells come in a variety of
shapes and sizes and play an important
role in protecting the body against

The hollowed-out disk shape of red
blood cells allows them to squeeze
through capillaries without damage.

infection and disease. All white blood cells have nuclei, and some also
contain large granules. Some of these granules contain **enzymes** that
can help destroy foreign invaders such as **bacteria** and **virus** particles.
Some cells surround these invaders and destroy them, and some
develop a "memory" of invaders so that a swift defense can be mounted
if the they invade again. Other white blood cells kill bacteria and
infectious agents.

Platelets

Platelets are disk-shaped cell fragments even smaller than cells. They
stop blood loss from cuts by forming platelet "plugs," and their granules
contain chemicals that make the blood clot.

BLOOD GROUPS AND BLOOD TRANSFUSIONS

The surfaces of red blood cells are made up of many different **molecules.** Blood is put into different groups depending on which molecules are present or absent. Blood grouping is important in **blood transfusions** and organ transplants, as red blood cells from different groups may stick together if they are mixed.

The major blood groups

The major blood grouping system is known as ABO. It was developed in 1900 by an Austrian doctor, Karl Landsteiner. Two of the different molecules that act as **antigens** may be found on the surfaces of red blood cells: antigen A and antigen B. A person's blood group depends on which of these two antigens are present on his or her red blood cells. The blood **plasma** also contains chemicals called antibodies, which can bind to antigens on the red blood cells. A person's plasma contains only antibodies that are not on his or her own blood cells.

Blood group	Antigen present on red blood cells	Antibody present in plasma
A	A	anti-B
B	B	anti-A
AB	A and B	none
O	neither A nor B	anti-A and anti-B

Mixing blood groups

If group A blood is mixed with group B blood, the plasma antibodies will bind to the red blood cells, making them stick together and form clumps. This is called agglutination. If this happened in the body, the clumps would prevent blood from **circulating** properly. The red blood cells may also become damaged and burst. It is therefore very important to match donor and recipient blood for a blood transfusion. Group O people can donate blood to people of any other blood group, because there are no antigens on the group O red blood cells to trigger agglutination. Group AB people can receive blood from any other blood group. They already have both A and B antigens, so there will be nothing new to trigger agglutination.

The Rhesus system

Another major blood grouping system gets its name from Rhesus monkeys, because the Rhesus factor was first identified in these monkeys. This antigen may be present on the surface of red blood cells. If you have Rhesus factor on your red blood cells, you are Rhesus positive (Rh+). If your red blood cells do not have Rhesus factor you are Rhesus negative (Rh-). If an Rh- person is given Rh+ blood, he or she will make antibodies against Rhesus factor and destroy the red blood cells. It is therefore important to match Rh groups for blood transfusion.

If an Rh- woman has a baby with an Rh+ man, their baby may also be Rh+. The mother's blood will mix with the baby's blood when her baby is born, and the mother will make anti-Rh antibodies. These will not harm the first baby, but if she has a second Rh+ baby, the antibodies in her blood will destroy the baby's red blood cells. Until recently, these babies needed an immediate blood transfusion at birth to save their lives. Now, the mother can be given an injection as soon as her first baby is born to prevent her from making the antibodies, therefore protecting any future Rh+ babies she may have.

The ABO and Rhesus systems are the most important blood grouping systems, but many more have been identified. They are not important in blood transfusions, but when patients receive organ transplants, they are matched as closely as possible. They are also potentially useful when deciding whether or not a man is a child's father, because blood groups are all passed onto children from their parents.

BLOOD DONORS

Blood is collected from donors and screened carefully to make sure it is free of disease. **Blood transfusions** are needed when patients undergo major surgery or when there is blood loss after an accident. Other patients may need just some components of blood, such as red blood cells or **plasma.**

Before people give blood, they are asked questions about their health, age, weight, and recent travel to other countries. Their blood is also checked to make sure that they do not have **anemia.** A donor sits or lies down, and the inside of the elbow is cleaned. A new, sterile needle is inserted into the **vein.** The other end of the needle is attached to a plastic tube that leads to a collecting bag. As the donor squeezes his or her hand, blood flows from the vein, down the tube, and into the collecting bag. Usually one unit of blood (one pint, or a little more than half a liter) is collected. The donor is then given something to eat, such as fruit or cookies, and allowed to rest.

Most people feel fine after donating blood. The body replaces the lost fluid within about 24 hours, and the red blood cells are replaced within a few weeks.

After collection, the blood is sent to a laboratory for testing. ABO and Rh groups are tested, and the blood is screened to make sure it is free of potentially dangerous diseases such as hepatitis, HIV, and syphilis.

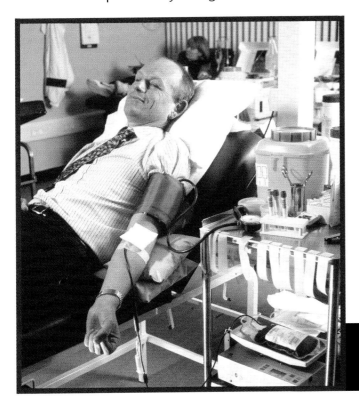

Separation of the blood

Blood can be used as whole blood, but because many patients need only some of its components, it makes sense to separate them so that several patients can benefit from one unit of blood. It is usually separated into:

- red blood cells—these can be stored in a refrigerator for several weeks or can be frozen for years. They can be used for treating anemia.

It takes about twenty minutes to donate one unit of blood.

- **platelets**—these are stored at room temperature for a few days only. They are used for treating leukemia and other conditions in which there is a platelet deficiency.
- plasma—this can be stored frozen for several years. It can be used to control bleeding, as it contains special chemicals that will help blood to clot.
- white blood cells—these must be used within 24 hours of collection. Doctors are still conducting research to find out how they might be useful to help fight infections.

Other products that can be taken from blood include clotting factors that play an essential role in controlling **hemophilia.**

This table shows the incidence of blood groups among population groups in the United States.

Unfortunately, there always seems to be a shortage of blood. But because there will always be illnesses and accidents, it is up to everyone to make sure that the blood banks are full. After all, you never know when you might need blood yourself!

Population Group	Blood Group (percentage)			
	O	A	B	AB
White	45	40	11	4
African American	49	27	20	4
Hawaiian	37	61	2	1
Inuit (Alaskan)	38	44	13	5
Asian American	40	28	27	5
Native American	79	16	4	1

HEMOPHILIA

Hemophilia is an inherited disease that affects the ability of the blood to clot—the blood either clots slowly or not at all. Because of the way hemophilia is inherited, it nearly always affects men and not women. People with hemophilia bruise very easily and badly, and even a tiny scratch can be dangerous, as the bleeding is difficult to stop.

Blood clotting

Blood clotting occurs as the result of a series of chemical reactions. Each step in the chain triggers the next one. The chain starts with Factor 12, which triggers Factor 11; Factor 11 triggers Factor 10; and so it continues until the last step in the chain, Factor 2 triggers Factor 1. The end result of this chain is the formation of a mesh of **protein** and fibers, which traps blood cells and forms a clot that prevents any more blood from escaping.

If any of the chemicals in the chain are missing, the whole chain breaks down and the blood cannot clot properly. The most common type of hemophilia is A, where Factor 8 is missing. In type B, Factor 9 is missing. In mild hemophilia the level of Factor 8 is lower than normal; in severe cases, it may be completely absent.

Detecting hemophilia

Severe hemophilia is often detected in young babies, because they bruise very easily. As they grow older, they may begin to bleed into their joints. This is very painful and can keep the joints from forming properly, which results in disability. Milder forms of hemophilia may not be diagnosed until the child is older, when bleeding from a minor cut continues for longer than normal.

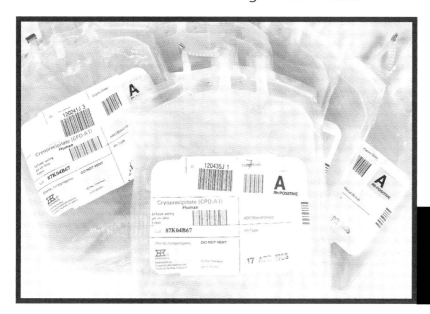

Blood tests determine the amount of Factor 8 in the blood and give an indication of the severity of the disease.

These blood products are rich in the blood clotting Factor 8, used to help control hemophilia.

Treatment

Until recently, there was no treatment for hemophilia, and it could be a very disabling disease. Now Factor 8 can be extracted from blood and injected into patients to prevent uncontrolled bleeding. During the 1980s many people with hemophilia developed AIDS after receiving donated blood containing the HIV **virus.** Strict controls are now in place to prevent this from happening again. Blood is screened very carefully to make sure that it does not contain any infectious agents and, as an extra precaution, all stocks of Factor 8 are treated to kill any HIV virus that may be present. Additionally, scientists have now found ways to produce Factor 8 in the laboratory. This method does not use blood from donors and therefore carries no risk of infection.

Inheriting hemophilia

Hemophilia is an inherited disease. This means that it is passed from one generation to the next. Looking at patterns in family trees over many generations has helped scientists understand how hemophilia is inherited. It is very rare for a woman to have hemophilia, but she can be a "carrier," which means that she can pass hemophilia on to her sons.

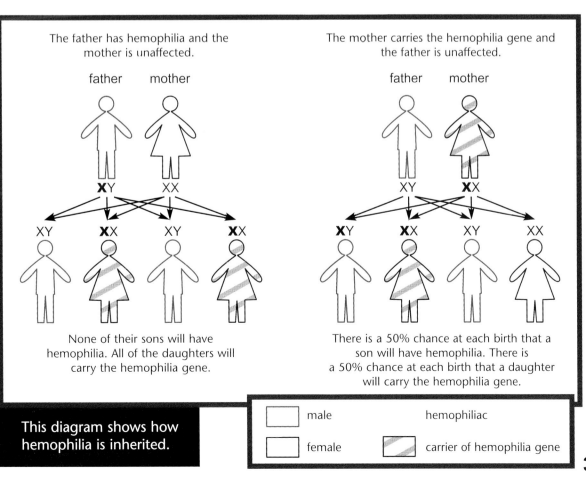

The father has hemophilia and the mother is unaffected.

father   mother

XY   XX

XY   **X**X   XY   **X**X

None of their sons will have hemophilia. All of the daughters will carry the hemophilia gene.

The mother carries the hemophilia gene and the father is unaffected.

father   mother

XY   **X**X

XY   **X**X   XY   XX

There is a 50% chance at each birth that a son will have hemophilia. There is a 50% chance at each birth that a daughter will carry the hemophilia gene.

| | male | | hemophiliac |
| | female | | carrier of hemophilia gene |

This diagram shows how hemophilia is inherited.

BLOOD DISORDERS

Blood plays an important part in maintaining every organ and tissue in the body. Any disorder of the blood itself can therefore affect the rest of the body. There are a variety of things that can affect the blood.

Anemia

When a person has **anemia** his or her blood cannot carry as much oxygen as it should. He or she feels tired and lifeless, and the skin often looks pale. There are several possible causes of anemia:

- heavy loss of blood due to injury or internal bleeding
- lack of iron, because the diet does not contain enough iron or because the body does not absorb it properly. Good sources of iron include meat (especially liver), eggs, shellfish, some vegetables, beans, nuts, and fruits.
- failure of **bone marrow** to function properly, usually due to poison or radiation
- bursting of red blood cells, for example by a **malarial parasite**
- immature red blood cells due to lack of **vitamin** B_{12}. Good sources of vitamin B_{12} include meat, milk, cheese, and eggs.

The most common cause of anemia is lack of iron, and this is usually treated with iron tablets or iron injections. Because some of the major sources of iron are meats, vegetarians and vegans have to be particularly careful to ensure that their diet includes enough iron.

Leukemia

Leukemia is a cancer of the blood. There are two main forms of leukemia:

- myeloid leukemia, which starts in the bone marrow
- lymphocytic (or lymphoblastic) leukemia, which starts in the **lymphatic system.**

Either type may be acute—which means it develops very rapidly—or chronic—it develops more slowly and is less serious. In acute leukemia, two things happen. First, white blood cells do not mature properly, so they cannot fight infection. Second, too many white blood cells are produced, so they clog up the bone marrow, preventing it from working properly. They spill into the blood, liver, and **spleen,** where they cause even more problems.

Patients suffering from leukemia often have anemia, because their bone marrow is unable to make enough red blood cells. They are also susceptible to infections, as their white blood cells cannot work properly. And they often bleed and bruise easily, because they do not have enough **platelets** to clot the blood.

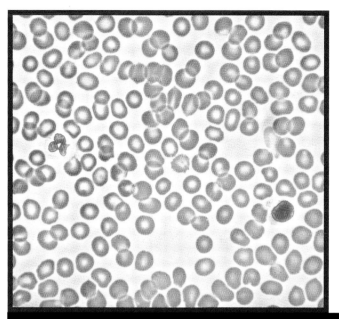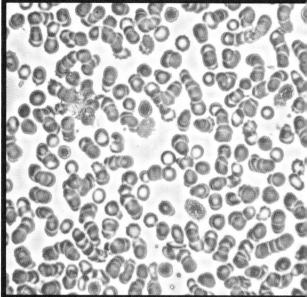

The photograph on the left shows normal blood. The photograph on the right shows the blood of someone with leukemia. There are many more white blood cells (shown in blue) in the blood of the person with leukemia.

Leukemia is usually treated by chemotherapy, which uses drugs to kill the white blood cells. The bone marrow can then grow again and operate properly to produce normal white blood cells. **Radiotherapy** can also be used to stop the production of white blood cells.

Bone marrow transplants are sometimes used to treat leukemia, if a suitable donor is available. A brother or sister is the best donor, as his or her cells are likely to be most closely matched to the patient's cells. This minimizes the risk of rejection of the transplant and the risk of the transplanted cells attacking the patient's body.

Bone marrow transplants

In a bone marrow transplant, the patient's bone marrow is first treated with drugs and radiation. Bone marrow is then sucked out of the donor's pelvic bones and filtered to remove unwanted cells before being injected into the patient's bloodstream. The transplanted cells find their way into the patient's bone marrow, where they take over the production of healthy blood cells.

When there is not a suitable bone marrow donor within a family, a search is conducted countrywide and sometimes worldwide. Lists of people willing to donate are kept, with details of their tissue types, so that when donors are needed they can be contacted quickly.

Sickle cell **anemia** is an inherited disease that affects red blood cells, causing difficulties with transport of oxygen around the body. It is more common among some population groups than others and can be diagnosed by a simple blood test.

Sickle cell anemia affects the red blood cells. The **hemoglobin molecules** become long and stiff, bending the red blood cells into a sickle shape. These sickled cells do not carry or release as much oxygen as healthy red blood cells do, and they also burst easily. New red blood cells cannot be formed as quickly as the sickle cells burst, and so the person develops anemia.

Treatment

People with sickle cell anemia may not know they have the condition until they suffer a "crisis." The sickled cells block small blood vessels, preventing normal blood flow and causing pain, especially in the bones and joints. During a crisis, a person will be given plenty of fluids and oxygen, if needed. Transfusions of healthy red blood cells can be given, although the patient will continue to produce their own sickled cells, too. A **bone marrow** transplant can be very beneficial, if a suitable donor is available.

Because of the poor oxygen transport, other symptoms of sickle cell anemia include tiredness, weakness, and an increased likelihood of catching coughs, colds, and other infections.

Much of the treatment for sickle cell anemia can be carried out at home. Parents need to help young children, but teenagers can often deal with their medicines and treatment themselves. Medicines need to be pumped into the body regularly. The medicine can be delivered by way

This photomicrograph shows the deformed blood cells of sickle cell anemia.

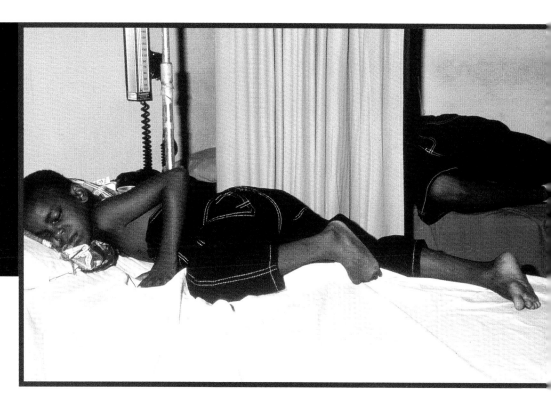

Sickle cell anemia is most common in areas of the world where malaria is prevalent. This African boy is receiving hospital treatment for the condition.

of a needle attached to a small portable pump by a length of flexible tubing, so the patient can move around during treatment. Some may use the pump overnight. This way, they can receive their medicine while they sleep.

Some patients need **blood transfusions,** and this means a trip to a hospital. Healthy blood from donors can help reduce the effects of the sickle cell anemia. For children and teenagers, this can mean a lot of time off school. To ensure they do not fall behind with their work, facilities are usually available so that they can study and do homework while they are at the hospital.

Sickle cell anemia and malaria

Sickle cell anemia is most common among people who live in areas where **malaria** is **prevalent**—particularly people of African and Caribbean descent but also in those from India, Pakistan, the Middle East, and Eastern Mediterranean areas.

Sickle cell trait is not the same as sickle cell anemia. It rarely causes any health problems and, in countries where malaria is common, it can actually be beneficial. The blood contains high levels of potassium, and this kills the **malarial parasites**.

WHAT CAN GO WRONG WITH MY HEART AND BLOOD?

This book has explained the function of the heart and blood, why they are important, and how they can be affected by injury and illness. This page summarizes some of the problems that can affect young people. It also gives you information about how each problem is treated.

Many problems can also be avoided by practicing good health behaviors. This is called prevention. Getting regular exercise and plenty of rest are important, as is eating a balanced diet. This is especially important in your teenage years, when your body is still developing. The table shows you some ways you can prevent injury and illness.

Remember, if you think something is wrong with your body, you should always talk to a trained medical professional, such as a doctor or school nurse. Regular medical checkups are an important part of maintaining a healthy body.

Illness or injury	Cause	Symptoms	Prevention	Treatment
Anemia	Heavy loss of blood, lack of iron and vitamins, red blood cell problem.	Feeling tired and lifeless. Skin usually looks pale.	Eat a diet rich in iron and **vitamins.**	Iron tablets or injections. Medical causes need specialist treatment.
High blood pressure	Hardening and thickening of **artery** walls, reducing their elasticity.	Virtually none, so often goes undetected.	Maintain a healthy lifestyle.	Weight loss if obese; increase exercise; low-fat diet; stop smoking; decrease stress; possibly drug treatment.
Heart attack	Blockage of the coronary arteries.	Chest pain; pain in the left arm; sweating; difficulty breathing.	Maintain a healthy lifestyle.	Rest; drug treatment; possibly surgery.

Illness or injury	Cause	Symptoms	Prevention	Treatment
Raynaud's disease	Constriction of **arterioles** in fingers and toes, usually in response to cold, restricting blood supply.	Cold and white fingers; intense pain.	Keep hands and feet wrapped. Avoid moving suddenly from hot to cold conditions.	There is no cure, but special gloves and socks can prevent extreme cooling.
Varicose veins	Smoking or lack of exercise; standing for long periods.	Dark, knotty threads visible beneath the skin; swelling, pain, and cramps in the lower legs.	Maintain a healthy lifestyle.	Wear elastic stockings. Drugs or surgery may be necessary.
Phlebitis	Injury or infection of a vein, which leads to inflammation.	Swelling and discomfort; a red streak along the line of the **vein.**	Maintain a healthy lifestyle.	Rest and wear special stockings. Possibly drug treatment.
Thrombosis	Blood clot blocking an artery, stopping blood flow.	Heart attack if coronary artery blocked; stroke if artery supplying the brain is blocked.	Maintain a healthy lifestyle.	Drugs to dissolve the clot.
Deep vein thrombosis (DVT)	Blood clot in a deep vein due to poor circulation, heart disease, varicose veins, or lack of exercise.	Tenderness or sharp pain in the leg, fever, and a rapid heartbeat.	Avoid knee socks that restrict blood flow, rest with feet raised, wear special stockings, keep moving.	Drugs to make the blood less "sticky."

Further reading

Bankston, John. *Robert Jarvik and the First Artificial Heart.* Bear, Del.: Mitchell Lane Publishers, Inc., 2002.

Gold, John Coopersmith. *Heart Disease.* Berkeley Heights, N.J.: Enslow Publishers, 2000.

Viegas, Jennifer. *The Heart: Learning How Our Blood Circulates.* New York: The Rosen Publishing Group, Inc., 2001.

# GLOSSARY

aerobic using oxygen

anemia condition in which the amount of hemoglobin in the blood is reduced

anaerobic not using oxygen

antibiotic drug used to fight infections. Antibiotics destroy microorganisms, such as bacteria or fungi, but are not effective against viruses.

antigen chemical that can cause a response by blood cells

aorta main artery carrying blood away from the heart

arteriole blood vessel formed by the branching of an artery

artery large blood vessel carrying blood away from the heart

atrium (plural is **atria**) one of the upper chambers of the heart

bacterium (plural is **bacteria**) type of microorganism

bacterial infection invasion of body tissue by bacteria, which then reproduce themselves within the tissue

blood clot clump of blood cells and other debris that may block a blood vessel and prevent blood from circulating freely

blood transfusion transfer of blood from one person to another

bone marrow soft tissue at the center of some bones, where blood cells may be produced or fat may be stored

capillary very fine blood vessel

carbohydrate nutrient that is broken down to release energy

cardiac having to do with the heart

cardiopulmonary resuscitation (CPR) method that may be used in an emergency to help a person who has stopped breathing and whose heart has stopped beating

cholesterol fatty substance found in some foods

chromosome part of the genetic material found in every cell in the body

circulation movement of blood around the body

collagen protein that makes up many structural parts of the body.

defect fault that prevents something from working properly

deoxygenated having had the oxygen removed

embolism blood clot that blocks an artery

enzyme protein that causes or speeds up chemical reactions

fibrin protein that is involved in the process of blood clotting

genetic having to do with the passing on of characteristics from one generation to the next

grafted attached to

hemophilia condition in which blood does not clot properly

hereditary able to be passed on from one generation to the next

hormone chemical made in the body that travels around the body and affects organs and tissues in a variety of ways

immune system body's defense mechanism against infection and disease

local anesthetic drug given to make a part of the body numb

lymphatic system network of vessels and glands that forms the body's main drainage system and is also involved with immunity

malaria disease caused by infection from a microorganism transmitted by mosquitoes

malarial parasite microorganism that causes malaria

membrane thin covering layer of tissue

mineral one of a number of chemicals needed by the body in very small amounts, for example calcium and iron

molecule smallest unit or particle of a substance made of two or more joined atoms

nutrient part of food that the body can use for energy, growth, or repair

oxygenated having had oxygen added

pericardium membrane that surrounds the heart

plasma liquid part of blood

platelet particle involved in blood clotting

prevalent common or widespread

protein complex chemical that is a component of many of the body's structures

pulmonary having to do with the lungs

pulse flow of blood through the arteries felt with each heartbeat

radiotherapy treatment with large doses of X-rays or other radiation to kill cells

spleen large abdominal organ involved in the formation and destruction of blood cells

solute solid that has been dissolved in a liquid

stroke blockage of an artery affecting the blood supply to the brain

systemic having to do with the whole body

valve flap of tissue that prevents backflow of blood

vein large blood vessel that carries blood back to the heart

ventricle one of the lower chambers of the heart

virus very small microorganism that can cause infection

vitamin one of a number of complicated chemicals needed by the body in very small amounts, for example, Vitamin C

INDEX